REVIVAL!
IT CAN TRANSFORM
YOUR CITY!

REVIVAL!
IT CAN TRANSFORM
YOUR CITY!

C. PETER WAGNER

WAGNER
INSTITUTE
FOR PRACTICAL MINISTRY
Preparing Tomorrow's Church Today

Revival! It Can Transform Your City!
Copyright © 1999
by C. Peter Wagner
ISBN 0-9667481-8-2

Published by
Wagner Institute for Practical Ministry
P.O. Box 62958
Colorado Springs, CO 80962-2958

Rights for publishing this book in other languages are contracted by Gospel Literature International (GLINT). GLINT also provides technical help for the adaptation, translation, and publishing of Bible study resources and books in scores of languages worldwide. For further information, contact GLINT, P.O. Box 4060, Ontario, CA 91761-1003, USA, Email: glintint@aol.com, or the publisher.

TABLE OF CONTENTS

CHAPTER ONE

CROSSING THE THRESHOLD OF REVIVAL: REVIVAL HAS COME AND IS COMING!

I would imagine that we have heard more revival reports in the last three to five years than we have heard cumulatively through the rest of the twentieth century. At this writing, I have 54 books on revival in my personal library, and the great majority of them were written in the 1990s. Christian people in churches from all kinds of theological streams seem to be talking about revival more than they ever have before.

REVIVAL IS GOOD

I don't recall ever hearing people speak disparagingly about revival. It is something that every Christian whom I know thinks is good—like a raise in pay or a faithful spouse or less crime or a delicious meal. Therefore in a day like today, when the subject of revival is a hot topic, expectations rise tremendously. Has revival really come? Are we seeing signs that revival is around the corner? Do people really know what they are talking about? Will I still be alive when the big re-vival comes?

This chapter's subtitle is "Revival Has Come and Is Com-ing." What I mean by this purposely enigmatic phrase is, first of all, that we do live in a season of genuine revival. But even so, it is not the Revival, capital "R," that we hope to see fur-ther down the road. In fact, I would express more confidence than that. As I see events unfolding and as I hear what the Spirit is saying to the churches, I have become bold enough to speak of the Revival not only as a hope but as a reality that most of us will actually see in our lifetimes.

If this is the case, we will be a generation that actually crosses the threshold of revival—the kind of revival that can literally and measurably transform our cities.

REVIVAL HAS COME

Revival is nothing new. There were revivals among God's people recorded in the Old Testament and launched by such legendary individuals as Jonah and Hezekiah and Josiah and Ezra and others. After Jesus left the earth, the spread of the gospel began with a revival on the day of Pentecost. This fulfilled Joel's prophecy that "I [God] will pour out of My Spirit on all flesh" (Acts 2:17). Peter saw revival when, after healing a paralyzed man, "all who dwelt at Lydda and Sharon saw him and turned to the Lord" (Acts 9:35). Paul saw re-vival in Ephesus when unusual miracles were happening and "all who dwelt in Asia heard the word of the Lord Jesus, both Jews and Greeks" (Acts 19:10).

As we turn the pages of history we read about revivals under the Montanists, Patrick of Ireland, the Waldensians, John Wycliffe and John Huss, John Welch of Scotland, Count von

Zinzendorf, Jonathan Edwards, John Wesley, Charles Finney, Evan Roberts of Wales, and on and on.

In our own decade exciting revival reports have come from Argentina under Carlos Annacondia, Omar Cabrera, Claudio Freidzon and others; from Brisbane, Australia under Neil Miers; from Toronto, Canada under John Arnott; from Holy Trinity in Brompton, England under Eleanor Mumford; from Mexico under David Hogan, just to name a few.

The United States has not been bypassed. Several college campuses have been experiencing revival during the 1990s, including Howard Payne University, Houston Baptist University, Wheaton College, Stanford University, Hope College and others. In 1995, an extraordinary year, revival was sparked by Randy Clark at the Tabernacle Church in Melbourne, Florida; another broke out later that year at Cal-

---

THE REVIVAL THAT WE HAVE BEEN PRAYING FOR
AND THAT WE LONG TO SEE IS AN OUTPOURING OF
THE SPIRIT OF GOD THAT WILL VISIBLY
TRANSFORM OUR CITIES.

---

vary Temple Worship Center in Modesto, California under pastor Glenn Berteau; in that same year the largest and most sustained revival in our nation began in the Brownsville Assembly of God Church near Pensacola, Florida under Stephen Hill and John Kilpatrick; and also in 1995 revival started at Harvest Rock Church in Pasadena, California under Ché Ahn.

We live in a time when revival is actually happening, so that is why I have asserted, in our subtitle, "Revival Has Come."

WHAT EXACTLY IS "REVIVAL"?

I have been using the word "revival" as if everyone agreed as to what revival really is. If I were teaching a course on revival, I suppose I would have to spend an entire class session discussing different people's definitions. Some draw a sharp line between "revival" and "spiritual awakening." In his excellent book, *Seasons of Revival* (BT Publishing), Frank Damazio distinguishes between "revival," "renewal," and "reformation," then goes on to quote definitions from Martyn Lloyd Jones, J. Edwin Orr, R. A. Torrey, Charles Finney, Andrew Murray, and others.

I have worked my way through many suggested definitions, but the one I like best comes from Richard and Kathryn Riss's book, *Images of Revival*. They say, "A revival is a sovereign work of God in which God pours out His Spirit upon all flesh."[1] This simple, uncomplicated definition reflects the language of Joel's prophecy fulfilled on the day of Pentecost (see Acts 2:17). The authors go on to describe many aspects of a true revival that deserve to be mentioned here:

- Revolutionary changes in lives
- Emotional excitement about what God is doing
- A vivid sense of God's presence
- Conviction to the most stubborn, obstinate unbelievers
- A new and refreshing atmosphere in the community
- Extended periods of worship
- Freedom in the Spirit
- New vitality to the church
- Repentance, conviction of sin, and awareness of God's judgment
- Secular media reports of what God is doing in the community

- A great harvest of new people coming into the church
- Visible manifestations of God's power
- Demonic deliverance and physical healings
- Extended prayer and fasting
- Unity of believers.[2]

REVIVAL IS COMING

This is not an exhaustive list of the characteristics of a genuine revival, but it will suffice for the moment. When you and I look at our cities, most likely we would say, "The things on that list are not happening to any significant extent where I live." That may be true, but they *should* be and I believe that they *will.* That is why I have said in the subtitle to this chapter, "Revival Is Coming."

The revival that we have been praying for and that we long to see is an outpouring of the Spirit of God that will visibly transform our cities. It will happen, I am convinced, but it will not be automatic. If we decide to take a passive, wait-and-see attitude, genuine revival will continue to be postponed. But if we decide to be active participants, if we decide to hear what the Spirit is saying to the churches, and if we decide to do whatever it takes to obey what God is asking us to do in these days, we will be the generation that sees the Revival with a capital "R."

The choice is ours!

Notes

1 Richard and Kathryn Riss, *Images of Revival: Another Wave Rolls In.* Shippensburg PA: Revival Press, 1997, p. 1.
2 *Ibid.* This list was gleaned from Chapter 1, "Characteristics Common to Revival," pp. 1–14.

———◆———

CHAPTER TWO

FROM CITY TAKING TO CITY TRANSFORMATION

This is a book about revival and city transformation. I explained a bit about revival in the last chapter, so now it is time to focus on the role that cities play.

There are several valid targets for our ongoing evangelistic efforts. An obvious one is individuals. Another is ethnic and language groups. Some may want to target certain religions or nations or areas of the world. However, in my opinion, the most important target right now is cities. The Holy Spirit seems to be saying that if we want to evangelize our nation, it will happen city by city. It is important, therefore, to see how revival can come to our cities.

TRANSFORMING CITIES

In 1990 John Dawson's book *Taking Our Cities for God* (Creation House) sold 100,000 copies. Since then just about every Christian leader has been talking about "taking cities." When

Ed Silvoso published his book *That None Should Perish* (Regal Books) four years later, he preferred the term "reaching cities," as reflected in his subtitle, *How to Reach Entire Cities Through Prayer Evangelism*. Now, however, there has been a change in terminology, spearheaded by George Otis, Jr., with a growing consensus that we should seek to "transform cities."

City transformation implies more than enthusiasm about the gospel, large meetings, stadium rallies, church growth, programs to help the poor, unity and good will among pastors, and so forth. A city that is truly transformed by the gospel will exhibit the characteristics of the kingdom of God here on earth. This is what we pray for when we say, "Thy will be done on earth as it is in heaven." The social, political, eco-

---

WE *CAN* HAVE REVIVAL IN OUR CITIES—
THE KIND OF REVIVAL
THAT TRANSFORMS
FROM TOP TO BOTTOM.

---

nomic, educational, judicial, racial, industrial, moral, ethical, and health conditions of the city will all change for the better. If it is going to happen, we must take the initiative. George Otis, Jr. says, "Transformed communities do not materialize spontaneously. If they did we might legitimately wonder why an omnipotent and ostensibly loving God did not turn the trick more often. We would also be left to ponder our own value as intercessors."[1]

Genuine city transformation might well look like the Northampton, Massachusetts of 1735 when revival came in the First Great Awakening under Jonathan Edwards. Edwards writes, "This work of God, as it was carried on, and the number of true saints multiplies, soon made a glorious alteration in the town; so that in the spring and summer following . . . the town seemed to be full of the presence of God; it was never so full of love, nor of joy, and yet so full of distress [i.e., fear of God's judgment among unbelievers—ed.], as it was then. There were remarkable tokens of God's presence in almost every house. It was a time of joy in families on account of salvation being brought unto them."[2]

COMMONALITIES IN TRANSFORMING CITIES

George Otis, Jr., author of *The Twilight Labyrinth* (Chosen Books), has been doing in-depth research on city transformation for some time. He has identified 18 cities in different parts of the world that are in more advanced stages of city transformation, and he has produced a fascinating video with the title *Transformations*. Of the 18, only one—Almolonga, Guatemala—can be classified as transformed, past tense. I will tell more about Almolonga later. Meanwhile, we are talking about stages of transformation.

Otis has developed a highly useful scale that divides the process of city transformation into three measurable stages with several subpoints under each of the three. They are: (1) spiritual beachhead, (2) spiritual breakthrough, and (3) spiritual transformation.

Among the 18 cities in advanced stages of the process, George Otis found five commonalities. The first two apply to 100% of these cities, and the last three apply to 90% of them:

1. Persevering leadership
2. Fervent unity of prayer
3. Social reconciliation

4. Public power encounters
5. Diagnostic research ("spiritual mapping").

JOHN DAWSON'S BOOK WAS THE KICKOFF

Since John Dawson's book was published in 1989, we have come a long way here in the United States. I liken his book to the kickoff in a football game. Throughout this decade we have advanced steadily. We haven't dropped the ball, but we're still not where we want to be. We are inside the 20-yard line, but we haven't scored the touchdown. Looking back, we have run some very decent plays. We have a good overall game plan. But the enemy is beefing up his line and he is prepared to do anything to stop us from getting that next first down, to say nothing about the touchdown.

ACUTE FRUSTRATION!

My perception is that we have entered a season of acute frustration in America. For nine years, at this writing, large numbers of the highest quality Christian leaders in our nation have placed city taking at the top of their agendas. In city after city something tangible is being done aimed at taking the city for God. These, for the most part, are not superficial efforts. Mission America, under the leadership of Paul Cedar, has included city taking among its highest priorities since the beginning. DAWN America, under Jack Dennison, has provided cutting-edge strategies in city after city, organizing, among other things, a high-level North American City Reaching Forum. Tom Pelton has been promoting Marches for Jesus in cities, and Steve Hawthorne has set a goal of seeing that every zip code is thoroughly prayerwalked. Jim Herrington is developing a new and promising paradigm for city reaching in Houston. David Bryant has been urging citywide Concerts of Prayer. Joe Aldrich has promoted Pastoral Prayer Summits, and Henry Blackaby has convened Solemn Assemblies in virtually every major city. Ed Silvoso has been pioneering prayer evangelism, holding regional City Reachers' Schools, and multiplying Lighthouses of Prayer. And I could go on...

Why the frustration? With all these high-powered, strenuous, well-designed, widely-supported programs for taking our cities, we haven't taken a single one yet!

BUT THERE IS HOPE!

Frustration is a fact. But what conquers frustration? Hope!

We *can* have revival in our cities—the kind of revival that transforms from top to bottom. We are inside the 20-yard line and the enemy is organizing a goal-line stand. But we can make the touchdown if we agree to do everything it takes to run five crucial plays. Those five plays are the subject of the rest of this book.

Let's do it!

Notes

[1] George Otis, Jr., "Community Transformation Through United and Persevering Prayer," *International Journal of Frontier Missions*, October–December 1998, p. 211.

[2] Keith J. Hardman, *Seasons of Refreshing: Evangelism and Revivals in America*. Grand Rapids MI: Baker Books, 1994, p. 65.

CHAPTER THREE

FIRST PLAY:
MOVING PRAYER AND SPIRITUAL WARFARE TO A NEW LEVEL

During the 1990s the prayer movement, on national and international levels, has made great strides. Unless I am mistaken, the logarithmic increase in both the quantity and quality of prayer over the past few years has been *the principal factor* in advancing us as far as we are now—inside the 20-yard line, to continue the football analogy from the previous chapter.

WE HAVE COME A LONG WAY

Here are some of the chief indications that we have come a long way in our understanding and application of prayer for revival and city transformation:

- Intercessors have been identified, raised up, trained, and empowered by the body of Christ. As few as ten years ago, we did not have a consensus that certain individuals have been gifted and called as intercessors. Our assumption was that every Christian should pray and that every Christian should be an intercessor, which is true. But we did not understand the crucial difference between Christian roles and spiritual gifts. Whereas every believer has the *role* of being a witness for Jesus, for example, God has selected a few to receive the *gift* of evangelist. Likewise, whereas every believer has a *role* to pray and intercede, God has selected a few to receive the *gift* of intercession.

It has now become common to ask an individual, "Are you an intercessor?" If he or she replies affirmatively, we know that such a person is different in many ways from the average believer. I have described the characteristics of intercessors in my book *Prayer Shield* (Regal Books).

- Pastors across denominational lines have come together in city after city with nothing on their agenda except to pray. They have frequently gone out of the city and spent up to three days together in prayer. This has now become the rule in American cities, no longer the exception to the rule as it was ten years ago.

- We have now begun to move our prayer efforts outside of our churches and into the community. We will always continue to pray in our churches, but now we realize that if we confine our praying there, our prayers will have mediocre effect on our cities. We didn't talk much ten years ago about Marches for Jesus or prayerwalking or prophetic acts or Lighthouses of Prayer.

- We have learned how to use a new arsenal of weapons for spiritual warfare. Ten years ago we did not even have the terminology to describe what God has been showing us, such as "strategic-level spiritual warfare," "spiritual mapping," "identificational repentance," and "commitment to the land."

Moving to a New Level

The past is wonderful, but it is not enough. The nearer we get to the goal line, the more the intensity increases. Some of our plays that previously worked well need fine-tuning because our opponent is now aware of them. A modern football team will watch videos for hours, just for the purpose of making the necessary adjustments so that their plays will be more effective than ever.

If we are going to score the touchdown, we must move to a new level in our application of prayer and spiritual warfare. Here are five areas that I see as crucial for our fine-tuning:

1. Partnership Between Pastors and Intercessors

Recognizing and appreciating the spiritual gift of intercession is an essential starting point. The next step is to affirm the *office* of intercessor. For years we have been comfortable with the office of "pastor" or "bishop" or "evangelist" or "elder" or "teacher." We are just recently getting comfortable with the office of "intercessor." Several churches I know issue name tags to intercessors, along with the other staff members, for use during their services. The name tag will say, "Sue Jones, Intercessor."

Intercessors are being given specific roles. For example, in some churches they are the only ones encouraged to minister in prayer one-on-one with strangers. In some churches they staff the prayer room. In some churches they organize the prayerwalking ministry. In some larger churches an intercessor might be added to the paid staff as Pastor of Prayer. Intercessors frequently pray through the services in another room. They lead prayer journeys. They are the ones people call in times of emergency.

All of this is happening, and it needs to happen more. But across the board, one weak link remains. A large number of pastors do not relate personally and positively to the intercessors in their churches. Some pastors remain ignorant that there are genuine intercessors in their congregation. Some are aware of them, but they do not trust them, much to the dismay and discouragement of the intercessors. True, some pastors have been burned in the past by flaky intercessors, but those wounds can and should be healed.

If I were the enemy, I would concentrate heavily on whatever it takes to keep pastors and intercessors apart, just as a defensive football team tries to keep the opposing quarterback and the wide receivers apart. To the extent that Satan has been accomplishing this, he has prevented the touchdown. I wrote my book *Prayer Shield* (Regal Books) to help pastors understand intercessors and to help intercessors relate positively to pastors. One of the reasons this book is now in its 17th printing is that many are finding it useful in making this essential connection.

2. PROPHETS HAVE NOT BEEN GIVEN THEIR RIGHTFUL PLACE

In the 1980s the contemporary gift and office of prophet began receiving wide recognition within the body of Christ. I believe that this phenomenon constituted the penultimate step toward getting the government of the church in place to receive the genuine revival that God wants to send. The final step was a parallel recognition of the gift and office of apostle in the 1990s. I will say more about this in a later chapter.

Because of the pervasive doctrine of cessationism (i.e., that the supernatural gifts of the Holy Spirit, such as prophecy, ceased with the end of the apostolic age and the close of the biblical canon), acceptance of the gift of prophecy was an extremely difficult step for many American Christian leaders to take. Many were trained to believe that God no longer spoke directly to His people. Jack Deere's book *Surprised by the Voice of God* (Zondervan) constitutes the intellectual *coup d'état* of cessationism, but a diminishing number are still holding out.

Prayer is now seen by most as a two-way conversation with God. We speak to Him, and He speaks to us. This is a very significant step forward.

However, even though cessationism may now be considered on the endangered doctrines list (if there is such a thing), it is still not easy for many ex-cessationists to move freely in a prophetic atmosphere. At a meeting of Christian leaders in a given city these days, it would be rare to find someone arguing that God no longer speaks to His people through prophets. Nevertheless, many are prepared to give only lip service to the prophetic movement. Receiving directional words for the city through mutually recognized prophets, and allowing those words to massage strategies and tactics, remains the exception and not the rule for city-taking programs. The voice of God has been muted.

Until it becomes the rule, we are not likely to see a touchdown in our city!

3. Pastors' Prayer Gatherings Have Lacked a Focus

We would not have reached the 20-yard line if pastors in cities had not started to tear down barriers between denominations and races and gathered together in fervent prayer. However, many of these pastors' prayer gatherings have lacked an agenda. This, at the beginning, was intentional because the focus of the meetings was to be on God and on Him alone. But it is clear that if we are going to move beyond just having prayer meetings to taking our city, *united prayer* must be driven by *united vision.*

These pastors' prayer gatherings have been one of the highlights of the 1990s. They have been universally acclaimed as one of the best things that has happened to the Christian community in the city. They have accomplished many things across the board, such as:

- Pastors have achieved unity of heart one with another.

- Pastors have repented to each other and remitted lingering sins of the past.

- Pastors have experienced personal renewal, and their ministries have reached new levels. Their people are blessed.

When I review that list, it occurs to me that what pastors have been doing is working out and getting in spiritual shape, the way football players work out to get in physical shape. They lift weights, they eat a high-protein diet, they adjust their helmets and shoulder pads to fit, they build up their stamina, and they get their picture taken. But suppose they did all this and went onto the field with no game plan? They would be asking for disaster!

This is one of the problems with a series of agendaless pastors' prayer meetings. Such meetings are fine for the fitness stage, but in the game you need a game plan. An agenda is absolutely essential.

There is a certain euphoria that often arises when pastors' prayer meetings first begin. "This is wonderful! We have never seen anything like this in our city!" But the outcome can tend towards making unity an end in itself. I like the way George Otis, Jr. puts it: "Pastors gather for prayer but their rendezvous are often lacking in passion. This is because emphasis is placed on corporate assembly rather than corporate vision. Trying to attract the widest cross-section of participants, they create an environment in which personal agendas proliferate like mushrooms. In the end unity is trumped by cordiality. Unable to achieve a common vision, they settle for a common place."[1]

Many pastors' prayer gatherings are structured to prevent any one person from "dominating," which is to say they prevent anyone from becoming the leader. Cities will not be taken for God without a leader whom the others have decided to follow. When the quarterback gets the team into a huddle on the 5-yard line, he does not ask the opinions of the other team members as to what the play should be. He does not seek a "consensus" before telling them what they will do to make the touchdown.

One of George Otis' "commonalities" in cities now enjoying advanced stages of transformation is "persevering leadership." The lack of persevering leadership has been a serious flaw in our city-taking procedures—one of the most serious!

4. WE HAVE BEEN SHOOTING IN THE DARK

Every church I know prays. Every church prays for individuals in the church, for families in the church, for the pastor and the church, and for the community in which they are located. Exceptions would be rare. In most churches that I know of, informed church members could tell about concrete answers to their prayers for individuals, for families, and for the pastor and the church. No problem. But very few could tell of equally concrete answers to their prayers for their community. In fact, in many cases they have been praying for their city for ten

---

SPIRITUAL MAPPING
IS TO INTERCESSORS
AS AN X-RAY
IS TO A SURGEON.

---

years, and their city is worse off now than it was when they started praying.

Why is this? The answer is very simple. If an individual asks me to pray for him or her, the first thing I do before praying is to ask, "What do you want me to pray for?" I may even ask the person another question or two before I pray. You do this, too. Why do we do this? It is because we have learned long ago that the more targeted our prayers are, the more powerful they seem to be.

Our problem is that we have not learned how to ask the pertinent questions about our community that will help us target our prayers for it properly. We have been shooting in the dark.

The tool to help us understand our communities as we ought is called "spiritual mapping." Spiritual mapping is to intercessors as an X-ray is to a surgeon. Without it we cannot do our best. A large number of Christian leaders involved in city-taking procedures know about spiritual mapping and affirm its value, but they are at a loss when it comes to actually doing it and gearing their prayer strategies according to what they learn.

Fortunately, help is available. My book *Breaking Strong-holds in Your City* (Regal Books) has helped many to understand spiritual mapping and lay a foundation. I am happy to announce that George Otis, Jr. has just produced the definitive textbook on the subject, *Informed Intercession: Transforming Your Community Through Spiritual Mapping and Strategic Prayer* (Regal Books). I recommend that leaders in every city get this book, digest its contents, and use the methodology it sets forth. If they do, we will move a lot closer to the goal line.

5. Local Church Prayer Is Largely Tokenism

I have reluctantly observed a serious defect in the prayer movement of the 1990s. With a few notable exceptions, prayer in local churches has amounted to little more than tokenism. I realize that some might question what I have just said, but those who want to check it out should start by looking at a church's annual budget. I do not have research on this, but I would guess that 90 percent of the churches in America have no line item for prayer in their budget. I am one who is inclined to press Jesus' statement literally: "For where your treasure is, there your heart will be also" (Mt. 6:21). If I am correct, we can therefore conclude that churches with no budget for prayer may well have little heart for prayer.

The fact of the matter is that most of the weight of the contemporary prayer movement has been carried by parachurch organizations designed to promote prayer ministry. I run one of them, the World Prayer Center. But at the same time I have a tremendous burden to see this situation changed, and to see local churches blazing the trail for effective prayer in our cities.

As a matter of fact, I think the Lord has given us a way to change the situation considerably. The mechanism that has emerged for local churches to access the databases and the breaking prayer information from the sophisticated technology of the World Prayer Center is to set up local church prayer rooms. If a local church dedicates a physical room in their facility for prayer, installs communication tools such as telephone, fax, and access to the Internet, designates a prayer room leader, and sets a goal of staffing the prayer room with intercessors up to 24 hours a day, they are eligible to join the Prayer Room Network and be linked, through the World Prayer Center in Colorado Springs, to all other local church prayer rooms across America and to 120 nations of the world.

This would, naturally, require an item in the church's annual budget. Among other things, most churches would send their prayer room leader to the annual Prayer Room Network Assembly in Colorado Springs in order for that person and the church to keep on the cutting edge of all God is doing in the prayer movement nationally and worldwide.

I am convinced that such prayer rooms will rapidly raise the water level of prayer in local churches across America, and release power for revival and city transformation that we have not previously seen.

Revival is coming!

Notes

[1] George Otis, Jr., "Community Transformation Through United and Persevering Prayer," *International Journal of Frontier Missions,* October–December 1998, p. 214.

—————◆—————

CHAPTER FOUR

SECOND PLAY:
FLOWING IN NEW STREAMS OF CHURCH ALIGNMENT

Just about every believer has heard the quote from Jesus: "He who has an ear, let him hear what the Spirit says to the churches." This exhortation is repeated seven times in the seven letters that Jesus sent to the churches in Asia Minor, recorded in the Book of Revelation, chapters 2 and 3. Let me make a couple of observations.

First, these letters were directed to the churches in seven different *cities.* This book is also directed to churches in cities, churches that are serious about doing whatever it takes to see revival and transformation come to their community.

WHAT THE SPIRIT SAYS TO CHURCHES

Second, Jesus referred to what the Holy Spirit is saying to the *churches,* plural. There undoubtedly are things that the Spirit is saying specifically to individual churches or congregations, but in many cases these words would not apply equally to other churches. However, when we hear things that the Spirit seems to be saying across the board to all churches, these are what should attract our attention.

The Holy Spirit is, indeed, saying some very important things to the churches here in the United States these days. If we are not aware of these things, it will be very difficult for our city-taking efforts to enable us to gain yardage, much less score a touchdown.

One result of the Spirit speaking to churches is that profound changes are taking place in regards to the way individual congregations and their pastors relate to each other.

PERSONAL RELATIONSHIPS MAKE ALL THE DIFFERENCE

I think the best way to summarize the heart of the new thing that is happening is to say that we are seeing a movement in church alignment from *bureaucratic organization* to *relational associations.* Everything is beginning to stand or fall on personal relationships. This means, among other things, that denominational affiliation, for many, may no longer be as important as it was in the past. Previously, most decision making was entrusted to *groups;* now we see more trust in *individuals.* And, as a result, we are acknowledging more personal authority than some of us have been used to. The new structures are not developed so much for *control* as for *coordination.*

City leaders who assume that everything today is just the way it always was cannot be as effective as they should be. When we are dealing with city transformation, we know that the agents which God will primarily use are the churches of the city. But if we are not aware of how the churches are relating to each another today, we will have one hand tied behind our back. We will be unsure as to whom we should talk to first or to whom we should listen the most. If we mislocate the centers of influence in the city we can find ourselves whistling in the dark. We must hear clearly what the Spirit is saying to the churches.

The new forms of local church alignment fall into four discernible patterns. Let's look into them one at a time.

1. INTRADENOMINATIONAL AFFILIATIONS

Intradenominational affiliations refer to new alignments of churches within the same denomination. Some pastors of local churches are beginning to feel that they can build more meaningful personal relationships with other pastors of their same denomination than with denominational officials such as district superintendents, executive secretaries of conferences, overseers, regional representatives, or bishops. Many feel that the obligatory meetings of presbyteries, associations, dioceses, or other forms of judicatories accomplish little more than informing pastors of what new decisions the denominational bureaucracy has made and what role the pastors are expected to play in implementing them.

THE MEGACHURCH PHENOMENON

Many of these new alignments, both intradenominational and otherwise, have been sparked by megachurch pastors. The megachurch phenomenon is a rather new feature on the landscape of church growth. I think that David Yonggi Cho of Korea was the major catalyst of the megachurch movement on the international scene, and that Robert Schuller of the Crystal Cathedral in Garden Grove, California was the major catalyst in the United States. Few knew about them in the 1970s, many did in the 1980s, and in the 1990s they now have many successful imitators. Megachurches have proliferated across denominational lines to the extent that we are now living in times when the influence of megachurch pastors within denominational families and in American cities is greater than we have experienced in previous generations.

Peter Drucker, known by some as the "father of modern management," says this about megachurches in a recent article in *Forbes* magazine: "Consider the pastoral megachurches that have been growing so very fast in the U.S. since 1980 and are surely the most important social phenomenon in American society in the last 30 years. There are now some 20,000 of them, and while traditional denominations have steadily declined, the megachurches have exploded."[1]

Megachurch pastors are a breed unto themselves. The simple fact that they preach to thousands every weekend and manage multimillion dollar budgets sets them apart from most. A major reason for their level of success is that they have unusual gifts of leadership. In addition, they are individuals of extraordinary vision. As mold-breakers and initiators, they have little motivation to implement plans made in a far-off denominational headquarters, particularly when those plans are seen as reinforcing the status quo.

Megachurch Pastors Face a Social Problem

Furthermore, megachurch pastors have encountered a new social problem. Although they may have resisted it, they face a widening social gap between themselves and fellow pastors of small- or medium-sized churches, particularly when those churches are not growing well.

I am stressing the social element because I am convinced that this frequent lack of rapport is not essentially attributable to spiritual qualities or to unfriendliness or to doctrinal issues or to nastiness or to desires for personal empire building. The fact is that when megachurch pastors meet with small-church pastors, their agendas are so different that they soon run out of things to talk about. Imagine, for example, the owner-operator of a local automobile body shop attempting to interact in any kind of depth with the Board Chairperson of General Motors, and you will have the picture. It is virtually impossible for most pastors to relate to the enormous ministry visions of a typical megachurch pastor without an unavoidable tinge of envy or a lurking suspicion that such a leader must be com-

---

THE NEW APOSTOLIC REFORMATION IS BRINGING THE MOST RADICAL CHANGE TO OUR WAY OF DOING CHURCH SINCE THE PROTESTANT REFORMATION OF THE SIXTEENTH CENTURY.

---

promising the gospel or nourishing an ego fixation. This causes predictable social problems both within denominational circles and among the Christian leadership of a given city.

So, what is the alternative? It is very simple. Megachurch pastors seek out personal relationships with peers with whom they can comfortably hang out and with whom they have much in common. They can share their problems with, learn from, and laugh and cry together with these peers. When megachurch pastors gather, they add value to each other. They feel that the time is well spent.

Their first preference is to hang out with other megachurch pastors of the same denomination. They form what I am calling intradenominational alliances. With few exceptions, these ad hoc alliances are neither authorized nor encouraged by the denominational bureaucracies since they are frequently perceived, in many cases rightly so, as creating alternative power centers. For this reason, such fellowships are ordinarily not widely publicized. Sources inform me that these alliances exist among Southern Baptist, Assemblies of God, and Nazarene megachurch pastors, to name a few. In fact, I have been told that the Southern Baptist megachurch pastors for at least 15 consecutive years have informally selected the person who was later to be elected President of the Convention.

2. INTERDENOMINATIONAL AFFILIATIONS

When megachurch pastors cannot find the desired peer-level personal relationships within their own denominations, they naturally look elsewhere. Some national leaders, whom I have begun to call "horizontal apostles," have clearly perceived the need and have begun to call peer-level pastors together.

I think of Robert Schuller, who has convened Churches Uniting in Global Ministries. Bob Buford of Leadership Network also has been doing this for years. John Maxwell of Injoy has handpicked a group of pastors whom he judges to be winners or "eagles," and he gives them special one-on-one attention. These are not actual megachurch pastors for the most part, but they exhibit the latent characteristics of megachurch pastors and Maxwell is helping them to achieve that goal. Keep in mind that none of these associations has any desire to exercise *control* over those who voluntarily affiliate with them.

All of these associations and others are interdenominational. Part of what this means is that many pastors are now finding that their primary allegiance, accountability, and personal bonding are with pastors of other denominations than their own. In some cases they will more readily respond to overtures requiring time, energy, and money from colleagues in other denominations than from their own denominational superiors.

3. EXTRADENOMINATIONAL AFFILIATIONS

The intradenominational and interdenominational affiliations listed above, with some exceptions, embrace mostly megachurch pastors. The main reason for this, as I have said, is social, but there is also a financial consideration. The costs of these affiliations are rather high, and out of the range of many smaller church pastors. No subsidies are usually available for such gatherings, as they frequently are for denominational meetings.

Most of what I am calling extradenominational affiliations are territorial. By this I mean that they are affiliations of pastors ministering in the same geographical area, usually in a given city. We are experiencing a trend for pastors in an area to get together on a regular basis for the purpose of building personal relationships. This is not always the stated, overt purpose of the gatherings, but relationship is the glue that holds them together. The dynamics are different from the traditional city ministerial associations, which have as a stated purpose to represent the Christian community as a whole to the government or the schools or the business sector or the media. In many cities they are also different from the pastors' prayer gatherings that I mentioned in the previous chapter.

OLD WINESKINS AND NEW WINESKINS

In the old wineskin of ministerial associations, every pastor in the city is eligible for membership based simply on holding the position of pastor or priest. It is, in essence, more *rational* than *relational*. Members do not have to like each other or agree with each other's doctrine or support each other's ministry. Charismatic leadership (in the sociological, not the theological, sense) is neither welcomed nor needed. Presidents are elected on the basis of seniority or political correctness. The highest expectation for the leadership is to be a man or woman of peace and to maintain the status quo at any cost.

Those involved in the new wineskin of extradenominational affiliations frequently think that ministerial associations are boring and ineffective. Extradenominational groups usually do have one or more charismatic leaders who cast new visions and promote innovations. Those who join do so because they *do* like the leader or leaders and agree with the direction they are taking the group. Because these affiliations are based on personal relationships, many pastors are developing a deeper sense of loyalty to other pastors in the city across denominational lines than to pastors in their own denomination. In fact, some have said that they are losing interest in attending their denomination's national annual meeting.

The new alliances are most often smaller than the older ministerial associations, but their potential for effecting change and for being the groups whom God will use in sending revival and city transformation is considerably greater.

4. POSTDENOMINATIONAL AFFILIATIONS

Postdenominational affiliations are the rapidly emerging apostolic networks that are a central feature in what I have been calling the New Apostolic Reformation. The New Apostolic Reformation is bringing the most radical change to our way of doing church since the Protestant Reformation of the sixteenth century. It is the fastest growing segment of Christianity on every continent in the world in this season.

The literature on the New Apostolic Reformation is increasing rapidly. I have two books on it. One, *The New*

Apostolic Churches (Regal Books), includes chapters by 18 of the world's top apostolic leaders. The other is a 71,000-word textbook on the movement: *Churchquake! The Explosive Dynamics of the New Apostolic Reformation* (Regal Books). I also recommend Donald E. Miller's study of the Vineyard, Calvary Chapel, and Hope Chapel in *Reinventing American Protestantism* (University of California Press) and Ted Haggard's insider's perspective from the personal point of view of a new apostolic megachurch pastor, *The Life-Giving Church* (Regal Books).

I would think that there are not many cities in America without new apostolic churches. They are frequently so different from traditional churches, however, that the recognized and established Christian leadership in the city either is unaware of them or tends to ignore them.

This response can severely weaken city-transformation efforts, because the new apostolic churches contribute a sensitivity to and a respect for apostolic leadership that many traditional leaders cannot contribute. I will have more to say in the next chapter about apostolic leadership.

Meanwhile, suffice it to repeat that if our cooperative strategies for seeing revival and transformation come to a city are going to fulfill their potential, these new alignments of churches and their pastors and the influence they can exert must be understood and utilized in the process.

Contentment with the status quo will surely keep us from crossing the goal line!

Notes

[1] Peter F. Drucker, "Management's New Paradigms," *Next* (from Leadership Network), November–December 1998, p. 4. (Originally published in *Forbes*, October 5, 1998.)

CHAPTER FIVE

THIRD PLAY:
APPLYING THE MEANS
FOR SUSTAINING REVIVAL

Consider this: If the revival we have been praying for actually came to many of our cities now, we would likely fumble the ball. The revival probably wouldn't carry us across the goal line to score the touchdown because we wouldn't know how to get the right grip on the ball. In other words, we do not know what steps to take in order to sustain revival. Our revival could turn out a mere flash in the pan.

SUSTAINING REVIVAL

Honestly, we Christian leaders haven't known much about how to sustain a revival. In fact, we have hardly even thought about it or discussed it among ourselves. One of the reasons is that most of the literature on revival deals exclusively with what we should do to produce the climate for *beginning* a revival. That, naturally, must be the first step. But few authors go beyond this, mainly because few people in our generation have as yet experienced a sustained revival long enough to analyze it.

There is some mention of sustaining revival in the literature. Charles Finney has twelve pages on it in his classic, *Revival Lectures* (Fleming H. Revell). Happily, some of our contemporary authors are now beginning to raise the topic. I think of Richard and Kathryn Riss in *Images of Revival* (Revival Press), and of Frank Damazio in *Seasons of Revival* (BT Publishing), and of Roy Fish's chapter, "How to Keep the Fire Burning," in *Revival!* by John Avant, Malcolm McDow, and Alvin Reid (Broadman & Holman).

Most historic revivals have lasted a year or two or three. I am referring to the revival fire itself. Even the most famous ones, such as Azusa Street or the Welsh Revival or America's First Great Awakening, were relatively short. Some have seemed longer because of the inspiring literature produced on them and because the afterglow, as over against the fire, was sustained over some years. The whole Pentecostal movement, for example, emerged from the Azusa Street revival.

There are records of some longer revivals. The Indonesian Revival in the 1960s lasted four years. A revival in Scotland under John Knox's friend, John Welsh, in Ayr, Scotland lasted 16 years. At this writing the revival at the Airport Christian Fellowship of Toronto has passed the five-year mark and the revival at the Brownsville Assembly of God in Florida is in its fourth year. Undoubtedly, much about sustaining revivals will be learned from these outpourings if they continue for a longer time.

THE REVIVAL IN ARGENTINA

The current revival in Argentina is different. It began in 1982, and it continues strong today. I have been able to track this personally over its seventeen years. I have visited Argentina multiple times to see the revival firsthand. I have developed personal friendships with its top leaders. For me it is, therefore, the one revival model I can draw on the most to suggest means for sustaining revival. I'm sure that my list is not exhaustive, and that other means need to be understood and applied as well.

I highly recommend the book I edited with Pablo Deiros, *The Rising Revival* (Regal Books), because it contains chapters by all of the most prominent leaders of the Argentine Revival after my introductory chapter. I also recommend Carlos Annacondia's book, *Listen to Me, Satan!* (Creation House), for the best insider's story. The revival dates from the time of Annacondia's first public meetings in 1982. Careful study of these books will surface many primary and secondary means of sustaining revival. For the purposes of this chapter, I have selected only three, but the three I consider the most important.

1. FOCUS FROM DAY ONE ON WINNING THE LOST

Above all else, Carlos Annacondia is known as an evangelist. Most of his ministry has occurred not within the four walls of churches but out in the open air. He leases a vacant lot and he personally preaches to between 2,000 and 20,000 people for 30 consecutive nights, from 8 p.m. until midnight, sometimes extending the campaign to 40 or 45 nights. He is a layperson, the owner of a nuts and bolts factory, and he takes no money from his evangelistic outreaches. The pastors of all the churches in a given city or section of the city cooperate and fold the new converts into their churches. At this writing, Annacondia has seen more than 2 million lost people come to the Lord through his ministry.

Carlos Annacondia set the evangelistic tone for the Argentine Revival, and it has not deviated. Many other things have been happening as well, but the highest priority of the revival has been winning the lost.

REVIVAL NEEDS NEW WINESKINS

This has not been true of all known revivals. Some have presupposed that the existing body of Christ needs to be renewed first of all, and only then can we begin to evangelize. I would suspect that this thinking may be the principal ingredient in the spiritual fire extinguishers that tend to put out revival fires prematurely across the board. Revival in a city is new wine, requiring new wineskins. In most cases those new wineskins, formed by the influx of new converts, are what will carry the revival forward, not so much the efforts expended in trying to patch up the old wineskins.

Ché Ahn sees this clearly. In his book, *Into the Fire* (Renew), he includes a chapter, "Going from Renewal to Revival." In it he argues convincingly that renewal in itself is not revival, but that genuine revival can be measured by its evangelistic results both at home and overseas. This standard is quite different from measuring the power of revival by how much "carpet time" Christians spend night after night. Carlos Annacondia would agree.

I am now convinced that revival will likely not be sustained for a long period of time if its initial focus is:

- On unity
- On social issues
- On renewal
- On worship
- On holiness
- On prayer.

Any of the above, if prioritized on an equal basis with or over evangelism, can shorten the life of the revival. All of them are good, and all are essential to the whole revival package. However, Jesus did not come to earth *primarily* to solve social problems or to get more people praying or to make peace among the religious factions of the day. He came primarily to die on the cross and rise again so that people could have their sins forgiven and be saved. Moving with the heart of God will create the atmosphere for sustaining revival, and God's heart is to seek and to save the lost.

2. TAKING AUTHORITY OVER *ALL* THE FORCES OF THE ENEMY

The first time Jesus sent out a group of His disciples, other than the twelve, to do ministry in the world, He said, "Behold, I give you authority to trample on serpents and scorpions, and over all the power of the enemy" (Lk. 10:19). The leaders of the Argentine Revival think that Jesus' words can and should be understood literally in our world today. They apply this on two levels: They have extensive ministries of personal deliverance, and they regularly confront territorial spirits.

PERSONAL DELIVERANCE FROM DEMONS

Argentine revival leaders aggressively cast out demons. Since Satan is Public Enemy No. 1 of revival and city transformation, we can be sure that he is busy dispatching large segments of his demonic army toward any initial outbreak of revival that might appear on his radar screen. To imagine that genuine revival will be sustained over a long period of time without confronting and dealing with these demonic forces of darkness is to live in a dream world far from spiritual reality. Ignoring demons is one way to ensure that our quarterback's passes are easily intercepted!

I do not subscribe to the theory that demons are equally distributed throughout the human race. In other words, there are some places where demons are more concentrated and where spiritual darkness is heavier than in other places. I think that, generally speaking, there are heavier concentrations of demons in cities than in most rural areas. Within American cities, I believe that the heaviest concentration of demons plagues the inner city. We have little chance of seeing transformation in our cities if we do not concertedly and aggressively confront those demonic forces.

Unfortunately, very few churches or Christian organizations in the inner city—or in the suburbs, for that matter—have well developed ministries of personal deliverance. Many parachurch ministries focus on the inner cities, and I have read the descriptive literature distributed by several of them. They are tooled to provide medical or dental service, to give clothing to the homeless, to manage soup kitchens, to offer legal assistance, to help people find jobs, to tutor school children, to hold Bible studies, to staff day-care centers, to finance small businesses, to run crisis pregnancy centers, to play midnight basketball, and to do many other good things. However, I have yet to find a brochure advertising that their ministry *casts out demons.*

W.W.J.D.—What Would Jesus Do?

I would have a hard time imagining Jesus, if He were here in person, sending ministry teams into our inner cities without first instructing them to heal the sick and cast out demons! It should be the rule, as it is in Argentina. But in the United States, unfortunately, deliverance is the exception to the rule. A chief obstacle preventing this from happening is a doctrine, quite widespread in our country, that Christians cannot have demons and that it is wrong to suppose that any bona fide Christians would ever need to have demons cast out of them.

A NEED FOR POLEMICS

It has not been my normal practice to bring up such controversies. I was a very polemical writer until about 1980 when God clearly told me to stop engaging in polemics. So, for almost 20 years, I have assiduously avoided controversial disputes. I now feel, however, that God is telling me to deal with at least a couple of issues in more polemical tones than I have been accustomed to.

I was greatly encouraged to move into this area when I

I DO NOT THINK THAT CITIES ARE GOING TO BE TRANSFORMED UNLESS A SIGNIFICANT NUMBER OF LOCAL CHURCHES BEGIN TO SPECIALIZE IN HIGH-PROFILE, HIGH-POWER DELIVERANCE MINISTRIES.

---

read John Eckhardt's new book, *Moving in the Apostolic* (Renew). In his section, "Polemic Preaching," Eckhardt says, "Apostles have an anointing to defend and confirm the truth. They walk in boldness and proclaim the truth in spite of persecution and opposition. . . This is what the Lord is restoring to the Church. Don't let it surprise or confuse you."[1]

I feel that the notion that Christians are immune to demonization is not among those benign doctrinal issues for which we should develop a courteous consensus of tolerance, such as whether we think the rapture comes before or after the tribulation or whether we baptize only believers and not infants. Rather, I am now convinced that this doctrine is a distinct *obstacle* to revival and transformation in our cities. The sooner those who defend this idea reconsider it and change it, the better, in my opinion.

I like what César Castellanos of the International Charismatic Mission in Bogotá, Colombia does. At this writing his church is the fastest growing megachurch in the world, with 30,000 home cell groups, among other ministries. In his church, all new converts are required to go on a two- or three-day retreat outside the city for the express purpose of receiving deliverance from demons. In addition, I once heard Harold Caballeros of Guatemala remind us that Jesus likened evangelism to fishing for people. But when a fish is caught, the first thing fishers do is to clean it. Christians, for him, should also be cleaned, and demons that might be oppressing them should not be ignored.

DELIVERANCE IN THE YELLOW PAGES?

I do not think that cities are going to be transformed unless a significant number of local churches begin to specialize in high-profile, high-power deliverance ministries. I would like to see them advertised in the Yellow Pages one of these days! I would also like to see a widely-accepted system of credentialing proven deliverance ministers. In short, I believe that we need to take the ministry of deliverance much more seriously than we have.

This ministry can produce results. One of the most publicized cases of deliverance a few generations ago is known as "Blumhardt's Battle." This German Lutheran pastor, previously inexperienced in deliverance, went through an incredibly exhausting process in casting a demon out of a girl, and the dramatic episode was recorded in detail and published in a book. I mention this because Richard and Kathryn Riss relate it to community transformation. They say, "These events transformed the whole village. A tremendous revival broke out in which lives were changed, broken marriages were restored, enemies were reconciled, and people began to experience physical healings."[2]

Confronting Territorial Spirits

Argentine revival leaders have long been convinced that part of effective evangelization involves using the authority that Jesus has given us to confront and evict territorial spirits. This premise mirrors the axiom in contemporary warfare that we must control the air before we send in the ground troops.

In the United States, pastors and other church leaders first heard about territorial spirits around 1990. Unfortunately, many of them cannot yet confront territorial spirits in their communities because they are still arguing whether or not they exist. The devil has been making his defensive stand at the goal line, and no wonder we haven't been able to penetrate it.

"Listen to Me, Satan!"

In every one of his evangelistic meetings, Carlos Annacondia directly confronts, even taunts, not only high-ranking demonic principalities but Satan himself. His famous war cry is, "Listen to me, Satan! Listen to me real good!" which, at the proper moment, he shouts at the top of his lungs. When he does, demonic spirits manifest all over the place, and they are decisively defeated by the authority of the blood of Christ. Then the evangelistic harvest can be abundantly reaped.

3. Having the Apostolic Order in Place

In Argentina the apostles are widely recognized, and they have built close, family-type relationships among themselves. They love each other, hang out with one another, support one another, and pray that others will be more successful than they.

They are each other's cheerleaders. Envy, jealousy, and one-upmanship are not part of the social mix. With God's government in place, no wonder the revival has been sustained.

OUR MOST SERIOUS FLAW

I want to stress this, because I feel that our inability to recognize the God-ordained apostolic leadership of our cities may well constitute the most serious flaw in our city-taking procedures across the board.

To the extent that we are not operating in the divine government outlined in Ephesians 4:11, we will find ourselves working in an environment that God will not fully bless. Our problem has been twofold: (1) Many have been ignorant that there are such things as apostles of the city (as distinguished from apostles in the churches), and (2) Even if we know they exist, we do not have a well-developed process of identifying them and empowering them for ministry. This deficiency needs urgent attention.

TERRITORIAL COMMITMENT

This thought is fairly new. I wish I could set forth a tried and true methodology for identifying these territorial apostles, but as yet I cannot. I am fairly sure of one characteristic that they will have in common, however, namely *territorial commitment*. Bob Beckett has brought the need for territorial commitment to our attention in his excellent book, *Commitment to Conquer* (Chosen Books). It is a fact that probably 90 percent of local church pastors in America do not have heartfelt territorial commitment. I think almost 100 percent would have strong commitment to their *congregations*, but few have gone beyond that and developed equal commitment to their *cities*.

The apostles of the city will undoubtedly emerge from

among those who have made it known that they are located in their city for the rest of their lives. Such a commitment brings with it a divine authority in that city, an authority simply not held by those who lack a territorial bond. Furthermore, the percentage of megachurch pastors who are committed to their city is larger than the percentage of smaller church pastors with such a commitment. It will not be surprising, therefore, if a disproportionate number of those eventually recognized as apostles of the city are found among the megachurch pastors. I do not mean by this that all megachurch pastors are city apostles, or that all city apostles are megachurch pastors, but many of them will be.

FANNING THE FLAMES OF REVIVAL

If we make these adjustments in our game plan, we will be able to fan the flames of revival once the fire comes. The enemy might be making a goal-line stand, but if we are determined to do whatever it takes, we can—and will—break through and score the touchdown of city transformation!

Notes

[1] John Eckhardt, *Moving in the Apostolic*. Ventura CA: Renew, 1999, pp. 84–85.

[2] Richard and Kathryn Riss, *Images of Revival: Another Wave Rolls In*. Shippensburg PA: Revival Press, 1997, p. 7.

———◆———

CHAPTER SIX

FOURTH PLAY:
REEVALUATING CITY-TRANSFORMATION PROCEDURES

In what I have said until now there has been good news and bad news. The good news is that city-taking projects have been springing up and taking root in city after city across America, involving much of our finest Christian leadership. The bad news is that we haven't taken one as yet!

ALIGNING STRATEGY AND TACTICS

Jack Dennison of Dawn Ministries has brought to our attention that a serious weakness in our city-taking efforts to date has been employing too many tactics without a proper strategy. I agree. Our situation is like the coach of a football team designing a playbook full of the most ingenious plays ever known, but having no game plan. Such a team is unlikely to score. The difference between the plays and the game plan illustrates the difference between tactics and strategy.

What has happened in a given city is this: A group of

pastors—say, from the west side—who have been meeting together to pray for their city decides to move ahead. They have heard of a ministry that advertises their ability to provide tools for taking cities, and they invite that ministry for a training conference. The west-side pastors convince the ministry leader that they represent the city. The assumption is that the key city leaders will be trained in the conference and that they will all be on the same page. Therefore the word goes out afterwards that the conference has "impacted the city." However, another group of pastors on the east side actually knew little or nothing about this conference. They proceed to invite a different ministry to bring its specialty. Groups of north-side pastors and south-side pastors do the same thing.

The upshot is that, over a period of months or even years, the city has hosted many excellent tactical training sessions. Every one of them has been good. But they are all shooting in different directions, and the motivation and skills that they release into segments of the body of Christ are never integrated into an overall strategy. As a result, large numbers of people may have been "blessed," but little in the city has changed.

If we continue what we have been doing we will never get past the line of scrimmage. If we are serious about gaining yardage and scoring the touchdown, we must become clear on both long-term goals and short-term goals.

LONG-TERM GOALS

As I have said previously, we need to agree that our long-term goal is not simply city taking or city reaching, but city *transformation*.

What would this look like?

Let me answer that question with two examples, one from

a few centuries ago and one from the contemporary scene.

FLORENCE, ITALY

Savonarola was a famous Italian prophet and revival leader in Florence, Italy, who ministered a generation before Martin Luther started the Protestant Reformation. At one point he prophesied that the city ruler, the pope, and the king of Naples would all die within the year, and they did. That attracted attention! He also prophesied that God would punish Florence with a foreign invasion. When King Charles VIII of France did lead his army across the Alps in 1494, Savonarola, single-handed, met the French forces and persuaded them not to sack the city!

This story is told by Wesley Duewel in his excellent book *Revival Fire*. Duewel goes on to tell how Savonarola's prayers and prophecies and revival leadership transformed the city of Florence:

"The wicked city government was overthrown, and Savonarola taught the people to set up a democratic form of government. The revival brought tremendous moral change. The people stopped reading vile and worldly books. Merchants made restitution to the people for the excessive profits they had been making. Hoodlums and street urchins stopped singing sinful songs and began to sing hymns in the streets. Carnivals were forbidden and forsaken. Huge bonfires were made of worldly books and obscene pictures, masks, and wigs. Children marched from house to house in procession singing hymns and calling everyone to repent and empty their house of every 'vanity.'

"A great octagonal pyramid of worldly objects was erected in the public square in Florence. It towered in seven stages sixty feet high and 240 feet in circumference. While bells tolled, the people sang hymns and the fire burned, reminiscent of Paul's revival bonfire in Ephesus centuries before (Acts 19:18–20)."[1]

What a graphic glimpse of how revival can affect a city!

ALMOLONGA, GUATEMALA

My wife, Doris, and I have had the privilege of visiting Almolonga, Guatemala twice. God has been so highly glorified and exalted in that city of almost 20,000 that Satan is embarrassed and irate. He is so upset that he tried to kill us both times. The first time he caused our private airplane to crash! The second time he suddenly sent a fierce hurricane that required our airplane to make an emergency landing in a different part of Guatemala! Sad to say, within a few hours another private plane carrying missionaries did crash near the airport where we were originally to land, and eleven died.

Earlier I mentioned that, of the 18 cities identified by George Otis, Jr. as being in advanced stages of transforma-

---

IN ALMOLONGA,
PEOPLE WERE BORN IN MISERY,
LIVED IN MISERY, AND DIED IN MISERY. . .
NOW THINGS ARE DIFFERENT.

---

tion, Almolonga is the only one that can be classified as transformed.

The revival that has transformed Almolonga has been sustained for 25 years. In the early 1970s Almolonga was a city of degradation in every way possible. Alcohol reigned, and drunkenness was endemic. Men would drink up their wages and go home to beat their wives and children. On Monday mornings the streets would be lined with drunks laid out like firewood. Sleeping around was expected behavior. Disease flourished, and the extreme poverty of the city had cut medical services to a minimum. Violence ran rampant. Children couldn't go to school. Overcrowded jails forced construction of new ones. Natural disasters seemed to be attracted to Almolonga. The land was barren, crops constantly failed, and food was always scarce. In Almolonga, people were born in misery, lived in misery, and died in misery.

BREAKING THE POWER OF MAXIMÓN

The territorial spirit over Almolonga was Maximón. He was so powerful that he could make his wooden idol in nearby Zunil puff smoke from cigars placed in the idol's mouth. Maximón had total control, constantly receiving worship from the people who would lavish his idol with gifts and promise to obey him in everything, if only he would "protect" them.

Now things are different. Some 90 percent of the people of Almolonga are born again. The largest and most prominent buildings throughout the hills surrounding the city are evangelical churches. A new church facility accommodating 1,200 has been built right on the town square. The city is clean. People are bright and cheerful. Well-dressed children attend school and their families stay intact. Of the city's 34 barrooms, 31 have closed. Disease and sickness, now rare, can be treated with readily available medical help. Roads are named "Jericho Street" or "Jacob's Well Avenue," and the businesses call themselves "Garden of Eden Pharmacy" or "New Jerusalem Restaurant" or "Zion Barber Shop."

Poverty? It is a thing of the past in Almolonga. The farmers raise world-class vegetables, including cabbages the size of basketballs and carrots as large as a man's forearm. Their fields are now watered from below with artesian springs percolating from the ground. They deliver their vegetables from Southern Mexico to Panama in Mercedes Benz trucks—adorned with "Jesus Is Lord" mud flaps—which they purchase brand-new with cash!

The last jail in Almolonga closed nine years ago because there were no more criminals. Now remodeled, it is called "The Hall of Honor" and used for wedding receptions and other community events.

CASTING OUT DEMONS LIGHTS THE SPARK

What sparked this revival and city transformation in Almolonga? Twenty-five years ago the city held a few small, weak, struggling, and discouraged evangelical churches. Then a young worshiper of Maximón named Mariano Riscajché was remarkably saved. At that moment God spoke to him and called him into the ministry, as He did the Apostle Paul. It wasn't long before Riscajché was ministering to one of the numerous city drunks. Riscajché decided to take authority and cast out a demon of alcoholism, and the man was instantly born again and delivered. Word got out, and in a short time Riscajché had led 400 others to Christ, delivering each of them from the demons that had bound them for years. One of them was a high priest of Maximón named José Albino Tajez. The power of the territorial spirit had been broken, and the rest is history.

Not long ago, the Guatemalan equivalent of *Time* magazine, *Crónica Semanal,* carried a cover story under the title, "The Defeat of Maximón!" Hardly anyone in Guatemala does not know about the transformation of Almolonga by the power of God. This is one of the reasons that, at 45 percent (with some estimates considerably larger), Guatemala now boasts the highest percentage of born-again Christians of probably any nation in the world.

I think we can agree that nothing less than this kind of

transformation should be our long-term goal in every city.

Short-Term Goals

As we develop a strategy for taking our city, it is important that we learn to measure our progress. Are we going forward? Are we standing still? Are we falling behind? Up until recently, we have not been able to come up with very accurate answers to those questions because we did not have any standard measuring device. Fortunately, the situation is changing. George Otis, Jr.'s book *Informed Intercession* (Regal Books) gives us a tool to help us measure progress from beachhead to breakthrough to transformation, with several subdivisions under each level.

It is only as we seriously take measurement and conscientiously apply what we know that we can troubleshoot what might be going wrong. This process parallels how a football team watches videos of past games in order to make the constant improvement needed to be a winner. Until then, a sense of frustrating confusion can predominate, leaving us easily discouraged.

Apostolic Leadership

In the last chapter I mentioned how important apostolic leadership was for sustaining the revival in Argentina. It was the same for Florence, Italy and for Almolonga, Guatemala.

It could go without saying that properly relating tactics to an overall strategy also requires apostolic leadership on a citywide basis. Committees and forums and prayer summits and ministerial associations will not get the job done. Some anointed individuals who know how to hear from God and to make decisions benefiting all those involved need to be recognized, trusted, and empowered to design the game plan and name the quarterbacks who will call the plays. There is no special need that they be called "apostles," although I think it is better if they are. Meanwhile, until that term might be more widely accepted and understood, call them whatever.

Do what it takes to get a winning game plan and go for the goal!

Notes

1 Wesley Duewel, *Revival Fire*. Grand Rapids MI: Zondervan Publishing Company, 1995, p. 46.

———◆———

CHAPTER SEVEN

FIFTH PLAY:
SETTING A STANDARD OF
RADICAL HOLINESS

If the members of a football team refuse to exercise, if they eat and drink the wrong things, and if they stay up to party all night before the game, they have little chance of winning. They may have a top coach, an excellent game plan, and plenty of individual skills. But if they are going to win, they also must be at the top of their physical conditioning.

SPIRITUAL CONDITIONING IS A MUST

The church today is much like a poorly conditioned football team. Spiritually, many believers are not in winning shape. We may be inside the 20-yard line in our progress toward revival, but we may not have enough spiritual reserves left to draw on to complete the task. We have developed many spiritual skills in such areas as preaching, worship, deliverance, prayer, teaching, spiritual warfare, prophecy, divine healing, and evangelism. But without personal holiness in each individual life, all our skills will not take us past the line of scrimmage. The enemy is too strong.

Fortunately, the desire is growing within the body of Christ for more purity and holiness. Holiness rose to a high profile in the Argentine revival a couple of years ago when Sergio Scataglini received an anointing to impart holiness, which he is now doing far and wide. Holiness has been one of the strongest and most consistent emphases in the Brownsville revival near Pensacola, Florida. Many Christian leaders who previously did not particularly stress holiness are taking up the call. I am encouraged.

GOD IS HOLY AND WE MUST BE HOLY

The Bible says, "As He who called you is holy, you also be holy in all your conduct" (1 Peter 1:15).

The first part of this exhortation has to do with the holiness of God. I think we have done pretty well in recognizing and understanding that God is holy. But many of us have stumbled along rather weakly on the second part, namely personal holiness in our conduct and our daily lives.

Researcher George Barna recently studied the behavior patterns of Christians in the United States as compared to non-Christians. Here is what he found: "The Bible clearly states that true believers should be readily distinguished from non-believers by the way they live. Yet, the evidence undeniably suggests that most American Christians today do not live in a way that is quantifiably different from their non-Christian peers, in spite of the fact that they profess to believe in a set of principles that should clearly set them apart."[1]

When you first read that passage, it sounds rather shocking. But after you think about it for a little while, chances are you will soon be admitting, quite reluctantly, that it is all too true. The word for holy in the original Greek is *hagios,* which literally means "being set apart." If we are holy we are set apart both *to God* and *from ungodliness.*

THE REFORMED VS. THE WESLEYAN APPROACH TO HOLINESS

A principal factor causing our poor performance in the realm of holiness has been, in my opinion, the pervasive influence of the Reformed doctrine of sanctification throughout American Christianity. Reformed theology, in which I have been thoroughly trained, is outstanding in expounding the holiness of God. But when it comes to personal holiness on the individual level, it falls short. I was taught that I should strive to be holy and that I should advance in my progress toward that

---

I BELIEVE THAT THE POWER
OF THE HOLY SPIRIT WITHIN
US CAN MOVE US THROUGH A WHOLE DAY
WITHOUT SINNING AGAINST GOD.

---

goal throughout my life. But I was also taught that I would never make it, since I could never be God. The famous hymn "Holy, Holy, Holy, Lord God Almighty" includes a line saying, "Only thou [God] art holy." If only God is holy, no human being can be holy.

I am now of the opinion that the Wesleyan doctrine of holiness is a much more accurate way of explaining what the Bible teaches about holiness. A basic assumption is that God would not tell us to be holy in all of our conduct, as I quoted from 1 Peter 1:15, unless it was literally possible for us to be holy. I believe it is possible for us not only to yearn to be holy and to strive to be holy, but to succeed in being holy. I believe that the power of the Holy Spirit within us can move us through a whole day without sinning against God. And if this can happen for one day, it can and should happen day after day.

This does not mean that I can live a day without the *possibility* of sinning against God. "If we say that we have no sin, we deceive ourselves, and the truth is not in us" (1 John 1:8). Even though we pray every day, "Lead us not into temptation," the devil goes about like a roaring lion, and temptation may come. But temptation is not a sin, and we do not have to yield when it comes. We can have victory in our personal lives! At the end of the day, we can look back and say, "Thank you, Lord, for allowing me to live this day without sinning against You or against other people."

When We Sin, We Confess!

When we do sin (I did not say *if* we sin), we then have the ways and means to take care of it immediately. "If we confess our sins, He is faithful and just to forgive us our sins and to cleanse us from all unrighteousness" (1 John 1:9). We need not go from one day to the next with any unconfessed sin hanging around. Once we confess it, we are forgiven by God, but if we have hurt other people through our sin we also have to repair that damage, which sometimes takes a little longer. Nevertheless, clearing the slate and beginning a new day totally cleansed from sin not only is possible, but is clearly God's will for us.

I feel that I have said enough at this point to help set our sights on living a holy life as a permanent part of our lifestyle. I am not going to elaborate any more because I have recently written a small book with the title *Radical Holiness for Radi-*

cal Living (Wagner Institute Publications).   This volume is something you can easily read in one sitting, and it has the potential to change your life.

SCORING THE TOUCHDOWN

What that book can do is to make you very sure that you are in the proper state of spiritual fitness to participate fully on God's team for revival and city transformation.   If we all do this, combined with the other four "plays" I have described, our generation definitely will see the Revival with a capital "R," and we will begin to see our cities transformed by the power of God working through us.

My prayer is that God will help us to know His strategy, that we will be willing to run His plays, and that He will be glorified when we push the enemy back and cross the goal line!

Notes

[1] George Barna, *The Second Coming of the Church.* Nashville TN: Word Publishing, 1998, pp. 120–121.

What is
Global Harvest Ministries?

There are still two billion individuals who are not within reach of the gospel and who do not yet have a vital, indigenous church movement.

Global Harvest Ministries, under the leadership of Dr. C. Peter Wagner, unites existing national and international prayer networks in order to focus maximum prayer power on world evangelization; especially for the lost people of the 10/40 Window.

Working with Christian leaders all over the earth, Global Harvest is **seeking to bring together a massive prayer force** that is equipped, trained and focused for the fierce spiritual battles that will free millions of people from the grip of the enemy, and allow them to hear and receive the Gospel.

We are seeking those who will join hands with us in the following ways:

- **In Prayer:** Mobilizing intercession and prayer for the world's most spiritually impoverished peoples.

- **With Financial Help:** Monthly support is needed to mobilize this massive, worldwide prayer effort.

If you are interested in helping in these ways, or would like more information on Global Harvest Ministries please contact us at:

Global Harvest Ministries
P.O. Box 63060
Colorado Springs, CO 80962-3060
Phone: 719-262-9922
E-Mail: Info@globalharvest.org
Web Site: www.globalharvest.org

The Wagner Institute for Practical Ministry was initiated in 1997 to be a catalyst to "Prepare Tomorrow's Church Today."

The Institute is being built from the ground up to provide quality training for practical ministry. The emphasis is not just on events, but on a process that will lead to realistic implementation of the training provided.

Dr. C. Peter Wagner

Our goal is to see each member of the body of Christ fully empowered and functioning in their giftings and callings. We are committed to excellence by providing the body with well-known leaders who will target training in key issues for the Church.

Please contact us for a full list of resources, upcoming conferences, and services that will help equip you to fulfill the Lord's call on your life:

Wagner Institute
P.O. Box 62958
Colorado Springs, CO 80962-2958
Phone: 719-262-0442
E-mail: admin@cpwagner.net
Web Site: www.cpwagner.net

WORLD PRAYER CENTER

The World Prayer Center, located in Colorado Springs, is the international coordination center for a growing movement of people dedicated to praying for the good news of Jesus Christ to go forth into every nation, every tribe, every community in the world. Built with state-of-the-art computer and telecommunications systems, the World Prayer Center is designed specifically for people to pray. It is equipped with computers, telephones, fax machines, email and other communication technology to serve the body of Christ with informative and timely prayer notices. The World Prayer Center connects globally with prayer partners and prayer room networks who are dedicated to push into the invisible world for the lost

Linking Up With the World Prayer Center

There are two ways for direct electronic linkage with the World Prayer Center, and through us with intercessors and prayer movements around the world. Here they are:

1. **National Prayer Networks.** If you live in a country other than the U.S.A., your contact with the World Prayer Center will be through a National Prayer Network. For information on National Prayer Networks, please contact:

Rich Danzeisen
World Prayer Center
11005 Hwy. 83, #119
Colorado Springs, CO 80921
Phone: 719-262-9922 Fax: 719-262-9920
E-Mail: RDanzeisen@wpccs.org

2. **Local Church Prayer Rooms.** The World Prayer Center serves as the National Prayer Network for the U.S.A. While we will be linking up with the headquarters of the major prayer ministries in our country, the principal way for any interested individual to link to the World Prayer Center is

through their local church prayer room. This opens up the possibility for every congregation in America to move into a new level of prayer for their church family, for their community, and for the world.

What is a local church prayer room? It begins when a church of any denomination decides to designate a physical room in their church facility exclusively to prayer. They furnish it and decorate it comfortably and tastefully. They install at least one telephone line, although some have two or three. They install a fax machine and a computer with modems for email and Internet. They put an individual with gifts for prayer and intercession, combined with some organizational skills, in charge. This prayer room leader recruits a volunteer staff which will occupy the prayer room up to 24 hours per day, 7 days a week.

Naturally, most of the prayer requests will come from their own congregation, their own community, and even from other churches in the community. But they will  also be linked, through the World Prayer Center, with thousands of other local church prayer rooms in all states and with the National Prayer Networks around the world.

If you are interested in applying for membership in the Prayer Room Network or in receiving more information, please contact:

Bobbye Byerly
World Prayer Center
11005 Hwy. 83, #119
Colorado Springs, CO 80921
Phone: 719-262-9922 Fax: 719-262-9920
E-Mail: BByerly@wpccs.org

Other Books Available from Wagner Institute Publications:

- *Confronting the Queen of Heaven*
  by C. Peter Wagner
  This powerful book, which has already sold 12,000 copies worldwide, will help you understand clearly how to come against this dark spiritual power and contextualize it for your state or city.

- *Hard-Core Idolatry: Facing the Facts*
  by C. Peter Wagner
  This incredible book will clear away the foggy thinking about idolatry that has permeated churches today! Every believer needs this book.

- *Radical Holiness for Radical Living*
  by C. Peter Wagner
  This insightful book will open the way for you to move to new levels in your Christian life. You can defeat Satan's schemes and enjoy daily victory in your walk with God!

- *Ridding Your Home of Spiritual Darkness*
  by Chuck Pierce & Rebecca Wagner Sytsema
  This practical, easy-to-read book can be used by any Christian to pray through their home and property in order to close the door to the enemy and experience richer spiritual life. Includes a step-by-step guide to praying through your home and property.

- *Receiving the Word of the Lord:*
  Bringing Life to Your Prophetic Word
  by Chuck Pierce & Rebecca Wagner Sytsema
  This powerfully insightful book will help you hear the voice of God, develop a deeper understanding of prophecy, learn how to test a prophetic word, and experience joy in responding to God's voice.

To order, please call toll free **1-888-279-2307** or 1-805-644-9721.

For quantity discounts, please contact Peter Crain at
1-877-WAGNERI (1-877-924-6374) or 1-719-277-6748,
or send an email to: **WISales@CPWagner.net**.